CATHLAMET ON THE COLUMBIA

SACAJAWEA

Cathlamet *on the* Columbia

Recollections of the Indian
People *and* Short Stories of
Early Pioneer Days in the
Valley of the Lower
Columbia River

By THOMAS NELSON STRONG

BINFORDS & MORT, *Publishers,*
PORTLAND, OREGON

As my friend, Newman J. Levinson, Sunday editor of the Oregonian,
*originally instigated the publication of these tales, and has
given me much valuable advice and assistance, this
little volume is respectfully dedicated
to him by the author*

Table of Contents

Preface

MODESTLY does the author of these tales refer to them as perhaps of little worth; but he has made a work which though small in compass, shines with a quality that endures. It is an unusual book. It possesses savor and sincerity, exactness and charm. Pioneer incidents are told with the warmth that comes of long saturated experience. The Indian scenes are more somber, as befits the race, but related in mellow tones that make the almost forgotten aboriginal live. They embody rare facts of value to the historian and ethnologist. Over all broods the background of river and fir.

In this setting Thomas Nelson Strong was born on March 17, 1853, of New England antecedents. His father, William, came to Cathlamet as the first judge of Oregon territory; and it was after his father's associate and friend, Thomas

Nelson, that the boy was named. Scarcely does the author allude to this boy, and never by direct reference. But into the boy's make-up, and the man's, there entered indelibly both the transmitted strain of a standard of culture and breeding, and the influence of the surrounding forest, native, and frontier. It is this combination that gives the book its abiding quality of vivid sensitiveness and reality.

A. L. KROEBER.

Introduction

THE tales told in this little book came to the writer in many ways. Some of the scenes described he saw himself. Indians in their lodges and canoes talked freely to him, a little boy. Hudson Bay Factors and French voyageurs in their declining years had many stories to tell, and these were caught up by greedy ears. What is here told is but a little of the gatherings of many years of wilderness life with native hunters and exploring parties in the Pacific Northwest. They may be in themselves of little worth, and yet may help future generations of our children to better understand the life and atmosphere of a peculiar time, to better appreciate the crimson and the gold, and mayhap a little of the gray of the morning hour of the white man's day on the Pacific Coast.

THOMAS NELSON STRONG.

CATHLAMET ON THE COLUMBIA

CATHLAMET ON THE COLUMBIA

I.

Cathlamet

ATHLAMET, on the Columbia, was, from time immemorial, the center of the Indian strength on the lower river. The Indian lingered longer and the Indian blood is more conspicuous there now than at any other place between Portland and the Ocean. Chinook was a mud beach, a mere fishing station, but Cathlamet was an Indian town before Gray sailed into the river or Lewis and Clark passed by on their way to the sea. Here at the last gathered and passed away the Cathlamets, Wahkiakums, Chinooks and Cow-

3

eliskies. Here Anderson lived for a while, and here the Hudson Bay Company, having passed away, came Birnie, Roberts and Allan and other old factors and clerks of the company to end their days. It was early recognized as an Indian center, and is the only place of the Fish Indians to which Kamiakin condescended to send his messengers when he was organizing the Indian War of 1855. At its best it was the largest Indian settlement on the Columbia River west of the Cascades, and from the Indian stories must have numbered in the town itself from 500 to 1,000 people. Like all Indian towns it changed population rapidly, and when the whites first knew it, it probably had 300 or 400 inhabitants. Sauvie's Island occasionally had more Indians, but they were there only temporarily, digging wapatoes.

4

Queen Sally, of Cathlamet, was the oldest living Indian on the Lower Columbia in the late fifties and early sixties, and her memory went back easily to the days of Lewis and Clark when she was a young woman old enough to be married, which, with the Indians, meant about the age of fourteen. Seventy years is extreme old age for an Indian, and especially for an Indian woman, but Queen Sally was all of this. Judging from her looks she might have been anywhere in the centuries, for never was a more wrinkled, smoke-begrimed, wizened old creature. Princess Angeline, of Seattle, was a blooming young beauty beside her.

It gave one a far-away feeling, in regard to the event not warranted by the years that had passed, when from the cliffs above Cathlamet she pointed out the spot where the canoes of

Lewis and Clark were first seen. She said the Indians had been on the watch for them for several days, as news had come by Indian post of the strangers from the East. Lewis and Clark with their party came in the afternoon or evening, and were met by the Indians in their canoes at or a little above the modern town of Cathlamet and escorted to the Indian village, which was then on the slough below Cathlamet, at about the point where the saw mill now is. How long they stayed here she could not clearly tell. It was evident she confused their westward and eastward trips and also their winter stay at Clatsop with their stay at Cathlamet village. Twenty-five miles to wandering Indians is a bagatelle of too little importance to be considered in fixing a locality. It was a time of feasting, wonderment and council making. Lewis and Clark

6

were doubtless weary of Indians by this time, but the strange sights they saw will never be seen again.

II.

The Indian Village

THE village was made up of cedar houses thirty or forty feet long and fifteen or twenty feet wide. How they managed to split and cut out the cedar planks, sometimes twenty and thirty feet long, two to three feet wide and three to six inches thick, of which these houses were built, with the tools they had, is a mystery. With wedges made of elkhorn and chisels made of Beaver teeth, with flinty rocks and with fire, they, in some way, and at a great expenditure of labor, cut out the boards. The houses were well built, an opening was left along the ridge pole for the smoke to escape and there were cracks in the walls, but, excepting this and the door, there were no open-

8

ings. Unless destroyed by fire, these houses would stand for ages, as the cedar was almost indestructible. Each house was fitted to accommodate several families. Along the sides, which might be six or eight feet high, and along the rear wall were built beds like steamer bunks, one above the other. From the lowest of these bunks the floor of earth extended out like a platform four or five feet to a depression of a foot or two along the center of the lodge, which was reserved for the fire place.

Fully inhabited by Indian men, women, children and dogs, lighted up by the smoky fires, the lodge interior looked like a witches' cave. Men and women in all conditions as to toilet lay sprawled on the earth platform about the fire. In the bunks amid dilapidated furs were numberless half-naked children and coyote-

9

looking dogs. Along the ceiling hung dried salmon and strings of dried clams and roots. The smoke circled everywhere, and gave a misty look of vastness to the room, and through all like a solid atmosphere was the smell, the awful smell of the Indian lodge. Fires in an Indian village or an occasional abandonment were recurring necessities in Indian life. Flesh and blood, even of the Indian variety, could not long abide in one Indian encampment. From this as well as from the necessity of getting food, it came about that the Lower River Indian lived in his village for only small portions of the year. It is safe to say that Lewis and Clark either found a lodge that had been little used or slept away from the village. No sane white man, except under stress of dire necessity, ever slept in a fully populated Indian lodge that had been used continuously by them for any great length of time.

One of the strange sights that Lewis and Clark saw about this Wahkiakum village of Cathlamet were the burial canoes. The last of these were not destroyed until late in the fifties, and when Lewis and Clark came they were very numerous about the village and in the Columbia sloughs between the Elokomon and Skamokawa Rivers. The low, deep moan of the Columbia River bar, forty miles to the westward, is clearly heard at Cathlamet, and it may be due to this that these burial canoes placed high in the Cottonwood and Balm of Gilead trees were always placed with their sharp-pointed prows to the west. With every paddle in place, with his robes and furs about him and all his wealth of beads and trinkets at his feet, the

dead Indian lay in his war canoe waiting for the
flood of life which should some day come in like
the tide from the sunset ocean.

Considering the great value of these canoes
and the time it took to build one, it almost pass-
es belief that they would be sacrificed to a simple
belief in the future life. It is exactly as though
upon the death of a multi-millionaire of our
day all of his moneys, stocks and bonds should
be buried with him, his heirs renouncing the use
of all his accumulations.

The Chinook canoe of the lower river was a
beautiful thing and was as much a home of the
Indians as was the lodge. In Alaska the Indians
had good canoes, but nothing that for size,
model and finish equaled the Indian canoe of
the Columbia. These river canoes were of all
sizes, from the one-man hunting canoe that

could easily be carried, and which required an
expert to handle, to the large cruising canoe
forty or fifty feet long and five or six feet wide,
which could carry thirty or forty people and all
their equipments. The straight up and down
lines of the stern and the bewitching curve of
the bow were very graceful, and the water lines
of bow and stern have never been excelled. The
building of one was the work of years. It was
painfully hollowed out with fire and flint and
beaver-tooth chisel, was steamed within with
red-hot rocks and water, and was stretched to
exactly the right proportion and kept in place
by stretchers strongly sewed in. It was swift,
beautiful and seaworthy. Its only weakness was
in the places where the cedar wood was cut
across the grain to give the lines of bow and
stern. Here in a heavy seaway the canoe would

always work, and from here the canoe would sometimes split from end to end. Many a tragedy of the sea was due to this inherent weakness, for in these and the Alaskan canoes the Indians traveled the entire coast line of the Pacific, from the mouth of the Columbia northward to Sitka and southward to the California line, and even farther, and old Indians often told of clinging to the broken sides of the canoe when it had split, for hours, and even days, until the surf rolled them ashore.

III.

Indian Men and Women

THE Lower River Indians had no horses and no place to use them, but dogs they had a-plenty. Why they kept them except as sentries no one ever knew. They were miserable creatures without courage or hunting instincts, but no one could come within a hundred yards of an Indian lodge without being discovered, and in this probably lay their value to the Indian, for they were not eaten except in cases of necessity or upon ceremonial occasions.

The Indians in their canoes were fine-looking people. Arms, shoulders and backs were well muscled and proportioned, and they handled their poles and paddles with grace and

15

skill, but away from their canoes the effect was not so good. They almost uniformly had short, squatty legs, sometimes made crooked by continual squatting in the canoes, and this gave them a curiously top-heavy effect.

Compared with the Horse Indians of Eastern Oregon and Washington they looked weak and insignificant. They were not as warlike a people as the Horse Indian, and in a land battle would have had but a poor chance. Intellectually they were superior, and the Indians of Eastern Oregon complained that at the Cascades, where the native peoples met to trade together, they were uniformly outwitted by their salt-water brethren. Upon the water they were superior also, and no Indian of the plains could handle a canoe as the Salt Water Indian could. The women were short, squatty creatures, with a tendency to grow fat and wrinkled when they could get food enough to grow fat on; the wrinkles they acquired anyway. From fifteen to twenty the Indian girl was a warm-blooded creature, not at all bad-looking, but after this she aged rapidly; at thirty was old, and at forty fit only to tan buckskins and do heavy work. In their native state very few of them lived much beyond fifty. The treatment of them by the Indian men was brutal to a degree that white women can hardly realize. Nevertheless they had a great deal of influence, and while an Indian in a fit of bad temper might in the evening knock down his tired squaw and leave her lying in the ashes by the fire, the next morning she would be his mistress of the household as usual. It was astonishing what good women the native women were, and how patiently and honestly they toiled and suffered for their worthless husbands. Afterwards when the white men came, the chance to marry one of the King George men or Bostons was to an Indian woman a chance to enter paradise. No white husband was ever as bad as an Indian, and however drunken and worthless the white man might be considered to be by his own people, he was a marvel of husbandly virtues in the eyes of his native wife. His word was law, and to him she was faithful to the death. Long centuries of oppression made the Indian woman thankful for even a poor specimen of a man. Thrice happy was her lot when she was taken for wife by a decent white man. In her inarticulate way she greatly rejoiced and sacrificed herself for him gladly. There are many people in Oregon and Washington who have Indian blood in their veins, and few, very few, of them have ever had reason to blush for their Indian mothers.

IV

Indian Children and Boys

THE children that Lewis and Clark saw on the lower river were odd-looking creatures. The babies were strapped to boards and looked like miniature mummies of Egyptian times, but the older ones were ceaselessly active. They were little brown fellows with slender legs that upheld and rapidly carried about a protuberant stomach, apparently four sizes too large for the legs below and the head above. It is astonishing how much they looked like the pictures of Brownies in our children's picture-books. Amongst them the rate of mortality was high, and they grew up with the dogs as best they could; were fed, and in a fashion clothed and sheltered, and that was all. As soon

as the little Indian could run about he commenced to hunt and fish, and in mere love of
slaughter would frequent the streams and maim
and kill the salmon coming up to spawn. The
little creek by Cathlamet was a favorite stream
of the Fall salmon, and here the little Indians
would gather and spear fish until they were
weary of the sport, and would then in mere
wantonness throw their captures on the rocks
to spoil. At thirteen and fourteen the boys would
begin seriously to hunt for game. The old Queen
Anne muskets that they had in early days would
be carefully loaded, not a grain of powder or a
single shot would be wasted, for these commod-
ities in the early days were difficult to obtain.
In his little one-man canoe the youth would
silently paddle through the sloughs looking for
ducks and geese, of which there were countless

thousands. He never attempted to shoot on the wing, and would rarely fire at a single bird, but would maneuver for hours to get a chance to fire into a sitting flock at short range.

As the great flocks of wild fowl had then, as they have now, a most exasperating habit of lying in open water beyond gun shot, a favorite device with the Indian was to cover his canoe with green boughs so that it would appear to be a mere floating heap of brushwood, and lying in ambush under this the hunter would patiently wait for hours for the birds to come near or for a favoring wind to float him into their midst. An Indian enjoyed killing ducks and geese in this way. The stealthiness and the ease of it, both appealed to him, besides it meant many birds for one shot.

So strongly was the necessity for economy

in powder and shot impressed upon them that a young Indian about fourteen years old, seeing one day a large cougar about to cross a stream on a log, did not fire at him from the canoe, but crept ashore and hid himself at the end of the log until the cougar nearly touched the end of his gun, when he fired, and, in the words of Western Ike, "Blowed a hole in that cougar that a bull bat could a' flew through without teching his wings on either side." Spoken to about the risk he had taken the youngster said he couldn't afford to waste a load of shot, and had to make sure work. These old guns missed fire very frequently, and the little Indian's economy might have cost him dear, but to his mind life was about the cheapest of his possessions; it had never cost him anything. For large game shooting they would frequently make a slug for their muskets by whittling out a wooden plug the size of the interior of the gun barrel, and with this make a mold in damp sand, into which was poured the melted lead. The result was a fearful missile. It would not go straight for forty yards, but as it was never fired at such a great distance this made no difference, for by lying in wait or careful stalking the Indian would get so close in to his game that a miss was impossible. A bear slain in this way looked after his decease as if he had been hit by a section of Mount Hood in some "Battle of the Gods."

V.

The Indian Hunting

PPOSITE Cathlamet in the Columbia River is Puget Island, named by Vancouver's exploring party on its first trip up the Columbia, in 1792, and here the Indians hunted the deer in the low, marshy lands along the sloughs. In the early times, before they used guns, the bow and arrow were sometimes used, but generally the hunts were elaborate affairs and long lines of skirmishers drove the frightened deer into the inclosures or pitfalls, but after the traders came with guns and gunpowder, the same wary tactics and careful stalking were employed in deer hunting as in the pursuit of other wild game.

Across the river, beyond its two channels and

Puget Island, was high land again, and here is one of the most beautiful pieces of forest and one of the most striking slopes in all of the Coast Mountains. Commencing at Cathlamet Head, the unbroken ridge sweeps easterly to a point back of Westport, and between it and the Nehalem River, for miles, the hunter travels in a great fir forest and up a gentle slope until he reaches an elevation of about three thousand feet, and sees the Columbia River to the north and east, the Nehalem River to the south and the Pacific Ocean to the west. Looking at it across the river from the hill in Cathlamet by the Birnie house, the sweeping outline of this long slope presents one of the most graceful and impressive scenes on the Lower Columbia.

Here Wholiky and Scarborough and all the mighty hunters of the Lower Columbia hunt-

26

ed the elk and the bear and the long aisles of those magnificent woods have seen some stirring sights. To watch one of these thorough hunters track an elk was always a fresh delight. For hours he would go uphill and down and out and in, in devious wanderings. Here a little twig misplaced or a leaf pressed down, signs too faint for the inexperienced to even notice, would tell him when and where the great beast had passed. No bloodhound ever followed the track more persistently. After hours, perhaps, of this kind of work, the signs would grow clearer and easier to follow, and the hunter's eyes would grow keen and hot, step by step he would increase his speed, and piece by piece he would drop his wrappings and clothes. It was said of Indian Dick that he rarely had any clothes, to speak of, on at the death, and yet so perfect was his woodland instinct that he would afterwards retrace his tracks for miles and gather up every article.

It almost seemed as if the hunter had the sense of smell possessed by hunting dogs, but the Indians disclaimed this capacity and to their familiar hunting friends talked freely about the way they found the trail. One thing that helped them was that they were familiar with the lay of the ground and knew the runways and habits of the animals and could very nearly guess where any particular one was bound.

Where an elk had been feeding it was very difficult to follow him, and sometimes the Indian would make a short cut to find out where he had left his feeding grounds, and this made it occasionally necessary to look up the back track, but ordinarily it was a straight-away stalk for miles through the brush and heavy timber,

28

and the hunter generally followed in the exact trail of the animal.

At the beginning of a chase an Indian hunter like Wholiky or Indian Dick would often venture a prediction as to where the chase would end. "We catch him on Rocky Hill little way over there," or "on little creek," or elsewhere, and usually there was where he was found.

On ordinary ground the track could be readily followed and on hard rocky soil there was always enough dust or vegetation to retain some trace of the passage of so heavy an animal as a deer, elk or bear; a dislodged pebble, a turned leaf or a crushed blade of grass was enough. The marvelous thing about it was the quickness and accuracy with which these slight signs would be seen and interpreted. A white hunter following his Indian friend had plenty of time

29

to watch the process, and it was as interesting as the working out of a great puzzle. To an ordinary white man who knew little of the woods or of hunting, it was magic pure and simple.

The closing in of the native hunter on his game was a stirring thing to watch. Long centuries of hunting with bows and arrows, feeble, short-range weapons, had bred into the Indian the habit of getting close up, and his having a gun made no difference with his habit.

Carrying his body low crouched so that it seemed to glide along the ground like a snake, placing each step with noiseless certainty and going through the underbrush as quietly as a fish in water, the stealthy panther-like quality of the Indian here showed at its best, for, close to his prey, fairly vibrating with tense and subdued energy, the Indian of the chase was a very dif-

30

ferent looking creature from the Indian of the lodge.

On one occasion Indian Wholiky in the wood and heavy underbrush of the Nehalem Mountains crept up so close to a black bear that only the thickness of a tree separated them. Poor bruin was astonished and dead in the same moment. The black bear in his chosen habitat of thick brush is one of the most unapproachable of animals by stalking, and poor bruin had a right to be astonished.

31

VI.

The Forest Ways

FEW people appreciate how different the forest home of the Indians of the Lower Columbia was from the habitat of other Indian peoples and what effect this had upon them. Cathlamet was situated on the bank of the Columbia River and was in a mere notch cut out of one of the most remarkable forests in the world.

For hundreds of miles to the North, East, South and West, the Douglas fir, now called in the trade by the commonplace name of Oregon pine, covered the earth with a green mantle two to three hundred feet in thickness.

The growth of one of these forests was as good an example of the opulence of nature as

32

could anywhere be found. Over the bare ground caused by a burn or windfall thousands of the cones of the fir tree would be scattered from the adjoining forest. Chattering pine squirrels and birds and the winds would carry the seeds. The next year the ground would be green with tiny trees, little fairy things of which there might be dozens to every square yard. In four or five years the ground would still be green, but the carpet of verdure would be perhaps six or seven feet deep, and of the little tiny trees perhaps nineteen out of twenty would have been crowded to death, and so dense would be the surface of this green carpet that the lower limbs of the little trees, and many of the little trees themselves, shut out from all light, would be dying and falling away. For two hundred years the process would go on, each young tree vigorously reaching upward to keep its head in the sunshine but making no attempt to reach out sideways, for this was hopeless. Only the stronger trees survived the struggle and thousands died each year shut out from light and life by their stronger brothers. The lower branches dropped off farther up every year as the green pile of the fir carpet was lifted higher and higher on the vigorous young stems. In perhaps fifty or a hundred years from the time the seed dropped on the ground there would be a compact young forest of beautiful timber fit for the masts and spars of ships, each tree eighteen or twenty-four inches through at the ground, going straight up into the air a beautiful straight shaft of nearly the same size a hundred feet without a branch or leaf, and then for fifty or one hundred feet tapering to the top and leafing out into the sun-

34

shine. When the forest was fully grown this green mass of leafage would be two or three hundred feet from the ground, and the great stems of the trees six and eight feet in diameter, would stand like great brown corrugated columns one hundred or one hundred and fifty feet without a limb.

Looked at from above, from the top of some high hill, for instance, this continuous forest appeared like a great green carpet spread evenly over a great sea of mountains, and it extended over hill and valley for thousands of square miles along the Pacific Ocean. Looked at from beneath, the forest vistas looked much like the groined aisles of some great cathedral with sweeping lengths to be measured by miles instead of feet.

Since the coming of the white man uncounted millions of feet of lumber have been cut from this forest and fires have in places ravaged it and yet so immense is its extent and so vigorous is its power of renewal that it is today to the casual sightseer the same unbroken forest that it has been from the beginning.

This was the home and the hunting ground of the Indian of the Lower Columbia. Some parts of it he knew well but into other parts he would not go, and it was curious to see how the places where game and food were plentiful became familiar ground while the other places were invested with superstitious terrors. Along the rivers where canoes could go the Indian was at home, and along some of the prairies and smaller streams of the Willamette Valley, Indian villages and homes were established, but the forest itself was untouched and except where it was

36

hunted in was unknown and feared by the Indians.

Thunder storms are of rare occurrence in the Valley of the Columbia and hence the Indians were very much impressed by them when they did occur.

Jim Crow Mountain, near Brookfield, was a rough piece of country in which the hunting was poor. It was "Mesatchie Illihee," and so in time the Indians connected together what they thought was cause and effect. Jim Crow Mountain obtained the reputation of being a thunder blasted district and as being the chosen resting place of the gigantic Thunder Bird who so terrified the poor Indians with the flashings of its eyes and the mighty roll and thunder of its dark wings.

A part of the Upper Valley of the Wenatchee

37

above the lake had also the reputation amongst the Indians of the neighborhood of being "Mesatchie Illihee" and of being the haunt of evil spirits. The first surveying party of the whites that went through identified the evil spirits in clouds of mosquitoes, which at times made the place uninhabitable and undesirable by either men or game. "Mesatchie Illihee" meant only rough, bad or difficult country, but the Indian ghosts and hobgoblins seemed to like this kind of country, for they were always located in it by the Indian story tellers.

The forest was so vast that the multitude of animals and birds that roamed through and lived in it were completely out of sight, and it was quite a common experience for the early explorers and surveyors to travel through it for weary days without seeing more than a pine marten or a chattering squirrel. Lewis and Clark in their expedition followed the rivers and this and good fortune and judgment was all that saved the party from disaster, for hunters well equipped but unacquainted with the woods, have starved in these great forests.

The Indians tried no experiments and unless compelled wandered into no unknown country, and the old Indian trails on the Lower Columbia were few in number. There was a well known way for the Indians and Indian canoes from Chinook River to the Naselle and thence to Shoalwater Bay and another from Shoalwater Bay to Grays Harbor. There was an Indian trail from the waters of the Cowlitz River to Puget Sound and another around the Cascades of the Columbia; and in the Willamette Valley, owing to its more open character, horses were used and there were a great many trails to different points.

The trails used by the Indians who did not use horses were always made by the tramping of feet and were never cut out or graded in any way. They practically always went up the sharp points of the hills and along the backbones of the ridges, and this was done to avoid fallen timber.

Thirty-five years ago a young hunter was searching for deer in the little range of mountains between the Willamette Slough and the Tualitin Plains. It was an idle, easy hunting, more for the love of wandering than for the desire of killing, and in the Summer evening he sat down to rest and look around. Something peculiar about a vista in the woods attracted his attention and he observed it closely. Apparently an old trail, it tempted him to wander along it. For miles and miles it kept its course and soon it was clear that here was the old Indian trail from the Tualitin Plains to the Columbia River at Sauvie's Island. Overgrown with moss, covered with leaves and mold, it was still the old trail that in olden times had been trodden by thousands of moccasined feet. There were no choppings or blazed trees along it, and even the roots of the trees rounded and rubbed by the clinging clasp of soft, flexible feet showed plainly that they had not been trodden or marred by the heavy foot-gear of the white man. Every foot of the location and every sinuous turn of the old highway bespoke its origin and use. It was the old and fading signature of a dead people. So dim and spectral and yet so unmistakable, it was the rising of an Indian ghost.

Following along the shadowy trail, he soon reached the summit, from where he saw before him the valley of the Lower Columbia. The mountains to the Eastward, the great river in the foreground, the Willamette Valley stretching to the Southward and many miles of river and forest lighted up by the evening sunlight.

As the evening deepened the young hunter could by a very easy stretch of the imagination see along the path lines of bent Indian squaws, each carrying on her back by a strap about her forehead a heavy load, and some, too, with little babies in their funny little bound-up packing cases, and trooping merrily at their heels, the little elf-like, copper-colored children and the wolfish dogs, and occasionally with these, and yet apart as became his dignity, an Indian warrior foot-loose and comfortable.

It was a long procession and it had passed and repassed that way for hundreds of years, and now only the trail was left, but the trail told many things to any one who could see.

To understand the Indian migration you must know what they are traveling for, because the Indian life was spent in traveling. In this case apparently these Indians had not traveled this road for war or sight-seeing or pleasure. It had only been the old quest of food.

Immediately below the sightseer from this point lies Sauvie's Island, stretching for fifteen or twenty miles down the Columbia River, and this island, famous in the history of the Hudson Bay Company and of the pioneers, was a garden of the wapato, the Indian potato. The lakes and overflowed lands were green with its many arrow-shaped leaves, and here every Autumn the

Indians used to gather for the purpose of harvesting it, and the stores so obtained helped to feed them through the Winter.

On the river was also the gathering place for drying and smoking salmon. The Cascades on the Columbia and the Falls of the Willamette at Oregon City were great gathering places in the salmon season, but there were plenty of other streams where the salmon could be caught. It was preserved by drying and smoking, and from an Indian encampment in the olden time an odor used to float down the wind that was so pungent and characteristic that it could almost be seen. No real and truly pioneer who ever lived near the Indians can to this day catch the slightest whiff of ancient fish without seeing in fancy the Indian lodges.

The Indians near the Coast made trips to the

44

ocean for the native cranberry and for clams. These later were dried and smoked and so cured, with an abundant sprinkling of sand, were probably the most indestructible food known.

Along or near the Coast were also the favorite hunting grounds for elk. The meat of the elk and deer was cut in strips and dried over the fire, making what was known as jerked meat. Farther up the river the sweet, glutinous root of the camas was dried and packed for Winter food.

The black bear is a cunning berry eater, and there is no more curious woodland sight than that of this big bear sitting upon his haunches drawing down huckleberry bushes and with flexible lips and tongue picking off the tiny berries one by one; but even the black bear is a dullard in gathering berries compared with the In-

45

dian woman. They knew every berry bush and patch anywhere within reaching distance and knew just how and when to gather them, and Olallies (berries) formed a great part of the Indian food supply.

To the people who knew it the forest was a magnificent granary of food, and perhaps one of the most pitiful stories of the West is that of a party of Eastern men fleeing panic-stricken from anticipated starvation, leaving their comrades to die by the way, because a little snow flurry and a little hunger met them in the woods. The mountains and the great forest were strange and terrifying to them. Had they been Indians or Western and forest-trained men they would have come out at their leisure, hungry and thin, half starved and hollow down to their boots, perhaps, but still all together.

46

THE FOREST WAYS

So far as Indian tradition goes there was never any famine amongst the native tribes of the Lower Columbia. When Azrael took his chosen from amongst these Indians to the Happy Hunting Grounds he walked with them along other death-trails than the dreary one of starvation.

VII.

The Coming and the Going

HERE did the Indian of the Columbia River come from?

Crab Creek, on the great plain of the Columbia, in Eastern Washington, is one of the most remarkable streams in the Northwest. At its source near Medical Lake it is a mere brook, and here, in 1870, there were trout, little fingerlings, by the hundreds. A few miles to the Westward the stream disappeared in sand and basaltic rock. Again a few miles below it came to the surface a larger stream than at first, and with larger trout. For 100 miles went this peculiar stream in this way, now sinking and now rising, every reach of open water stocked with trout of appropriate size, until at a point a little below Moses Lake, south of the Grand Coulee and 20 or 30 miles from the Columbia River, it finally disappeared in a waste of sand and rock. Thirty years ago in its lower reaches fat half-pound trout went in schools, and as the engineers of the Northern Pacific Railroad passed by they had much argument as to how the trout got there, and as to how the right-sized fish got in the right-sized streams. But the question is still unsolved.

In some such fashion men speculate upon the orgin of the Pacific Coast aborigines. How came this people to be scattered along the coast and in the interior, each one in his proper habitat, and who were the Adam and Eve of the Chinooks and Cathlamets? It is an endless subject, for they were apparently a people to themselves and resembled no others, and perhaps the

49

answer of Chief Moses, of the Wenatchees, is as good as any. Riding by this self-same Crab Creek in leisurely fashion one Summer day, he was asked how the trout got in. With an indulgent smile for the youthful ignorance that prompted such a question, the old chief answered: *"Mika ticka cumtux caqua ucook tenas salmon chawco copa tenas chuck? Na, na, chawco, nesica tillicum be nesika cumtux yaca quansum mitlite."* (You want to know how the little salmon got into the little creek? No, no, they didn't get in. My people know, and I know, that they have always been there.)

Another curious question has to do with the scanty native population of Western Oregon and Washington when first known by the white men. The range was limitless and food abundant beyond measure. The country could have supported easily five times the number of native people that were on it. These Indians always claimed that they were once a populous and powerful people, but that in some way they had provoked the Divine anger and been destroyed, and this claim is undoubtedly based upon fact, and on this question, although there are uncertainties regarding the manner of the decimation of the Indians of the Willamette and Lower Columbia Rivers, we have something definite to go on. This decimation began before the first white settlers came, and was largely finished before 1830. None of the histories give any idea of the number of Indians who inhabited this region before historic times, and this can only be conjectured, but it is certain that once a commensurate Indian population filled Western Oregon from the Cascade Mountains to the

51

Pacific Ocean. Every aged Indian told stories of a time when the rivers were lined with villages and floated many canoes.

At Marr's Landing, about three miles below Castle Rock, on the Columbia, the river has in the last few years been washing away what is known as the island, and has uncovered the site of old Indian camp fires. These stretch in a long line up and down the beach. They are covered with two or three feet of loam, and on this fir trees a hundred years old have grown. As many as fifteen or twenty stone hammers have been found about a single fireplace, and these old charred fires are preserved as they were 200 years ago. One pathetic little relic found amongst the big stone hammers was a tiny little hammer and pestle, evidently playthings of an Indian child. On Archer Mountain, a mile or two west, are

52

what appear to be ancient fortifications that would have required many warriors to man. No village of this magnitude was known there by white men. In the days of Lewis and Clark there was only a scattering settlement near Castle Rock, and a migratory trading band at the Cascades.

The Indian flint factory at the Clackamas River suggests a large population, and Cathlamet was always a greater city of the dead than of the living. Between the Elokomon and the Skamokawa the sloughs were lined with the burial canoes of the dead, and as only distinguished men were so buried, this stood for a very large population, probably greater than that of the Bella-Bella Indian Village in British Columbia. These canoe burials were ancient to say the least. Cedarwood is almost indestructible, and

53

no living Indians knew the name or lineage of the dead or resented the resurrection that the white children accomplished in searching for Indian ornaments. They tumbled the bones out of the bed of loam and leaves that had gathered over them, and they were the bones of a hundred years gone. In sport the children put them together and speculated upon what manner of men they were, and the Indian children joined in the game, for the dead were the old, old people.

Below the Indian village the ground was black and the plough turned up countless skulls and bones with flints and Indian arrowheads, bespeaking long occupation and a numerous population.

Long before 1800 the Indian had evidently reached the height of his power and prosperity,

54

and when the white man came was already on the way to extinction.

The waning of the Indian power of the Lower Columbia is shrouded in mystery. Young Indian girls told the story of it in hushed whispers, and the old Indians spoke of it reluctantly. Had the Death Angel come in bodily form they could not have been more impressed. The wail for the dead, so they said, was heard all along the rivers, and no one even hoped for life when the slaughter was on.

The Indians named the chief instrument of destruction the "Cole sick." With the white man came the smallpox and the measles, but the "Cole sick" was neither of these. About 1820 and 1830 epidemics of the old disease swept among the remaining Indians, and historians are puzzled to give it a name.

One suggests that fever and ague came with the settlers, but the Valley of the Columbia was never a fever and ague country and the pioneers, however malaria stricken at the beginning, must have been thoroughly disinfected by their long trip across the plains. Others say that the turning up of the soil by the Hudson's Bay people at the farms at Fort Vancouver released malaria from the soil and this caused the epidemic, but the disease was here before the farms, and it was impossible that a disease which raged over hundreds of square miles could have come from so trivial a cause. It may have been the modern la grippe striking an unprotected people. Whatever it was no more potent angel of death ever visited an afflicted people.

The white man had no need of war or violence in his dealings with these Indians, nor did he employ them, for the "Sahalee Tyee," the Indian god, had struck before him.

After 1800 the smallpox, measles and consumption were always busy, and a death in the Indian village was a common thing. There was no doctor at Cathlamet, and in pitiful dependence upon their superior skill the Indians used to come to James Birnie and William Strong, the only white settlers there, and ask for medicine, which was always given them, although it was no inconsiderable burden to supply it.

But sickness in an Indian lodge was not to be checked by medicines.

57

VIII.

The Medicine Man

N addition to these medicines Indians of the higher circles had Indian medicine men. A sick Indian, a smoky lodge, a hundred Indians beating the roof with poles to a monotonous chant and dance, and a temporary maniac manipulating the sufferer with rattles and Indian trumpery, it was weird medical work, and soon transferred the Indian of the higher circles to the select circle of Abraham's bosom.

The Indian war dance has for the last one hundred years been practically unknown on the lower river. Occasionally some feeble effort was made to imitate it, but nothing was ever done that could for one moment be compared with the wild rush and frenzy of a genuine war dance about the campfires of the Spokanes and Cayuses. These were performances to stir the blood and raise the hair. Nowhere along the seacoast were there any war dances to speak of. Even among the Hydahs, Tlinklits and Chilcats of Alaska the war dance was a spiritless, tame affair. The medicine dance, however, an entirely different thing, was at its best among the Coast tribes.

There were reports of Indian lodges in Western Oregon that were two hundred and twenty-four feet long, but this is probably an exaggeration, and a lodge sixty or seventy feet long must have been a large one. In such a lodge in case of sickness of some distinguished person, would be gathered at night a hundred or more Indians. In the sunken place in the middle of the lodge cleaned out for this purpose, and between the two end-fires would be placed upon a mat the sufferer lightly covered with furs. Around the sides and ends of the lodge in double and triple ranks, each with a pole in his hands, would be placed every available Indian man, woman and child.

In Cathlamet the white children would sometimes join in and were always welcome. At a given signal from some master of ceremonies, the dance would commence by everybody, at first slowly, but afterwards more quickly, jumping up and down in their places to a loud chant of yo-o-o, yo-o-o, yo, the first two long drawn out and the last sharply cut off and shouted almost explosively. No one stirred from his position except monotonously to jump up and down with the pole held upright in both hands in front of him, so that the movement brought it into contact with the low roof in perfect time with the chant and the jumping, the movements being so timed that the poles struck the roof all together with the final "yo." The noise was deafening and the lodge would shake in every timber.

After this had gone on with increasing enthusiasm for a half hour or so and the patient was supposed to be sufficiently prepared and the evil spirit properly alarmed, a terrific noise would be heard in the darkness outside, and suddenly the medicine man and four or five assistants would come bounding through the door with howls and yells into the smoky interior. They looked like fiends, bodies naked, faces covered with a hideous mask, over which towered a frightful headdress, and in their

hands rattles, large cumbersome things deco-
rated with teeth and feathers. This dress varied
with different people and different medicine
men, but the one idea was to make it as hideous
and awe-inspiring as possible so as to impress
and frighten the demons who had wrought the
evil witchcraft upon the sufferer. Not for one
moment did the dancing, chanting or pound-
ing cease or vary in its monotony.

The medicine man howling dismally, circled
with great leaps and bounds about his patient,
in sporting phrase, "sparring for an opening" to
get to close grips with the evil spirit. Finally his
chance came. The spirit, invisible to all but him,
had been caught off his guard. He rushed in,
seized the sick man, and with hands and teeth
attempted to drag from him the demon that
tormented him. In the contest the patient was

62

tossed and roughly handled, for Indian devils come out reluctantly.

The performance lasted for hours, taking the greater part of the night and the assemblage was wrought up to frenzy; but the treatment stopped only because human nature could endure no more. With the smoke, noise and general atmosphere the interior of the lodge became unbearable and the physical strain was too great to be longer endured.

Sustained and soothed by this struggle with the evil one in his body, the sick man himself with patience and before many days generally gave up the ghost.

IX.

The Sweat House

THEY had another device that for quick dispatch was superior even to the personal treatment of the medicine man, and this was the Indian sweat house. No Indian man in his native state voluntarily or for the sole purpose of cleansing himself ever took a bath. He trusted to the rain or to the necessary swimming, to passing through the wet woods and grass or to mere dry attrition for all the personal cleanliness he deemed necessary. It created a sensation in the highest social circles of the Chinooks, therefore, when Duncan McDougall caused his Indian bride-elect to be thoroughly soaked and washed preliminary to the marriage ceremony, and the fact was considered of so much importance that history has gravely recorded it as one of the notable circumstances that attended that notable wedding.

History, however, in giving so much prominence to this fact, has done injustice to the Indian woman. She was by instinct more decent than her Indian master and under favoring circumstances was neat and clean. To her a bath, although rare, was not an unknown thing, and therefore the sweat house was not ordinarily for her.

To the masculine Indian, however, a hot bath seemed the greatest sacrifice he could make to the deities that ruled disease and death, and so it happened far back in the history of the race that some aboriginal genius with a talent for inventing great sacrifices invented and brought into use the Indian sweat house. They were not much used on the Columbia River near the ocean, but on the Cowlitz and Lewis Rivers, all along the Valley of the Willamette and on the Upper Columbia and its tributaries sweat houses were everywhere to be seen. They were little, mound-shaped structures like a flat, old-fashioned bee-hive, were perhaps four feet in height and five feet in diameter, the size and form varying a little in different localities, and were constructed on the banks of the cold running streams. They were made of willow branches, loosely intertwined after the fashion of a great basket upside down, without any opening except a hole in front of just sufficient size for a man to crawl in.

After the willow work was completed it was daubed over with clay, making an almost impervious hut. The inside dimensions were carefully calculated so as to accommodate one man, crouched into the smallest possible compass, with the necessary apparatus for a vapor bath, and the manner of its use was simple. After heating a number of large stones almost if not quite red hot the Indian, naked as the day he was born, and with a vessel of water, would crawl in and take the stones in also. Closing the door up tightly he would pour water on the hot stones until he was almost parboiled with the hot steam. After bearing this as long as he could the Indian would crawl out and without any preparation would plunge into the running stream. In this manner would be accomplished the second great medical treatment of the Indian.

This course was taken for any illness or in-

67

disposition, and would be taken even in mid-winter, it not being an unusual thing for a sick Indian after such a vapor bath to plunge into the water while snowflakes were whirling in the air and ice running in the river. Where the indisposition was slight or due only to an uncleanly life, the Indian would survive the treatment and be even benefited by it, and it was these cases that maintained its credit as a "good medicine" in the eyes of the tribe.

With measles, smallpox and other diseases of similar character it was almost sure to cause speedy death, but as the Indian did not discriminate and with cheerful patience took it for granted that the afflicted one if he died was fated to death anyway, it did not discredit the remedy.

Occasionally an Indian would kill a medicine

man, or, as was once done by a sorrowing chief of the Klickitats, lasso the unsuccessful doctor about the neck and with the lasso fast to the saddle bow, ride his horse at full speed until the medical head was separated from the body, but no fault could be found with the sweat house, which maintained its credit as a sovereign remedy until many years after the coming of the whites, and this accounts for the fact that measles amongst the Indians was about as deadly as the smallpox.

X.

The Sins of the Fathers

ITH the white man came whisky and death hand in hand, and with him came the subtle laws under which nature punishes infractions of its moral code, and these laws struck at the very source of life of the Indian people.

Lucy Quillis, one of several of the name, for it passed from one to another, was the little nurse in the white family. She was carefully taught, clothed and cared for. But in those days you might just as well have put a pretty little tiger cat in pantelets. On her part, with the very best intentions, she taught her infant charges the Chinook language, how to gamble in Indian fashion, and some other things.

70

THE SINS OF THE FATHERS

When she was fifteen or sixteen years old, after the fashion of the young girls of her race, she fled from the house with her lover, a most unworthy scamp, and so began the life which ended a few years later in all that was left of poor Lucy, a mangled, battered body, being gathered up from the floor of the madhouse and buried. The "madhouse" of the Lower Columbia and of Puget Sound was not in pioneer days a lunatic asylum or a female seminary, only a judicious combination of the two with unlimited whisky thrown in.

The Indian woman of the Northwest Pacific Coast was not a flower-garlanded maiden or a frivolous French soubrette or Light o' Love, as so many Indian romances depict her. There was in her from childhood up a certain gravity and sober earnestness which was the natural result of her sober, hard-working life. For unnumbered centuries the burden of the toil and responsibility of her people had been upon her shoulders, and so far as she had anything to think with, she was a thoughtful, earnest woman. Inarticulate and coy in the expression of her feeling to a degree that imposed upon people who did not know of the fires that glowed beneath, she was in reality alive and earnest and had great capacities for joy and suffering. Above all things she was a simple, law-abiding creature.

In the tribe, as a maiden, she obeyed without question the moral code such as it was, of her people. Married to an Indian husband she was his slave, and married to a white man and made acquainted with his moral law, for his wife, she would have passed through fire, torture and death before she would have gone one step out

72

of the straight path in which he desired her to walk.

There is not on record in Oregon history a single case of an unfaithful Indian wife of a decent white man, and in view of this one cannot recall some particulars of the history of those early times without a shudder or without taking a firmer hold upon a belief in a future life in which the crooked ways of this world may be made straight, for God seemed to deal harshly with the Indian woman.

The spectre of the Eve of St. John when he spoke to "Smaylho'mes lady gay," spoke to understanding ears, and when he laid his burning fingers on her fair arm with the declaration:

"That lawless love is guilt above,
    This awful sign receive"

and left there the scorched brand of guilt he

73

branded wanton frailty, but God's Angel of Punishment in his dealings with many Indian women laid his hand on innocent victims and no law protected them, no voice warned them, and they did not even know for what they were stricken.

It is difficult for the white men and women of this day to conceive of the Indian code of morals or to appreciate how perfectly it fitted their wandering life or to understand how trustfully and innocently the young Indian woman met the white strangers when they came. No exploring or hunting party, however difficult or arduous the journey, ever lacked Indian women to go with it, and no white man had any difficulty at any time in obtaining a companion for his camp or home, nor from the Indian point of view was there anything indelicate or immoral in this. It was the old custom of their race come down unquestioned from Adam and Eve and had the full sanction of parents and friends.

Nevertheless to this trustfulness and innocence the terrible physical punishment that had been evolved for a race of men who had been educated for centuries was ruthlessly applied, and to make the situation still more unhappy and apparently unjust, no remedial or palliative agencies were known to the victims. The cruel thing about the early history of Oregon was that the trader came so long before the missionary that death's work was largely done to the Indian woman before either knowledge or help could come to her.

One of the saddest sights of early days was that of young Indian women driven out of the lodges to live or die as best they could alone in the woods. The other Indians would be frightened at their sickness and in their fear knew no pity. Occasionally an old woman or a grandmother, whose life was considered of little value either to herself or her people, would go out with the stricken one and care for her.

Such girls would patiently live apart in some little hut or wickie-up and without a word of complaint would care for themselves as they best could. The pioneer white women were in the habit of taking out food and such simple remedies as they could think of to these poor creatures, and not knowing the nature of their illness or daring to come close to them, would place it upon a convenient stump to which the sick girl would come when her friend had withdrawn a little, and then the two would cheerfully visit together with ten or twenty yards of pure air between them.

Ordinarily, when white persons were about, when death came, the dead were decently buried, but occasionally the interment was as fearful as the sickness, and this was true of the victims of any disease that the Indian feared was infectious.

One Winter evening a good old missionary, telling in reflective mood his experiences on the Northern Coasts in a smallpox epidemic, told of sending Kathla, a young Indian girl who had contracted the disease, to a hut far outside the Indian village on a point in the bay where her old grandmother went with her as nurse, and how every morning he went in his canoe to a point of tide-washed rocks near their hut, and not daring on account of his people to go nearer, shouted out his instructions and left there their food and simple remedies.

The missionary then wandered off in his story into a general description of that awful time; how twelve canoes laden with Indians seeking help camped on an island in the bay and after some weeks only one canoe went paddling away; and how, when the scourge had passed, he sent out trusty men immune to the sickness and bid them bury the dead who were lying about in the forest with orders afterwards to destroy their own clothing and go a-hunting for six months longer before returning to the village, so as not to bring the infection back with them.

The old missionary told of one old Indian who had contracted the smallpox and who insisted upon having his grave dug in advance

78

and his bed placed over it so that he could drop handily into it when he died, and added, in a chuckle, that the old Indian did not die after all and the grave was wasted, and then he lapsed into silence, forgetting that he had left Kathla's story incomplete, until some one asked about it.

With an effort of the memory recalling the circumstances, the good man answered as if it were an ordinary occurrence of those old days:

"Kathla and her grandmother, poor creatures! Oh, the wolves took them!"

This is the seamy side of Indian life and the process of extinction of the Indian was grim in spots, but strange as it may seem, this period of fifty or one hundred years during which the natives of the Lower Columbia were passing away, was not on the whole an unhappy time for them. The Indian took life day by day and did not worry for the future. Sheltered and with enough clothes and food he was happy. The individual was never seriously sick but once. The life and the medical system insured this and the fear of death was not in them.

One of the most pathetic characteristics of all the Indians on the Pacific Coast was their submission to what seemed the inevitable. A sick Indian gave up at once and died with no more fear or apparent suffering than if he were falling asleep, and his relatives buried him with low wailings, the sorrow of which died out with the echo.

To this day in Alaska the dying Indian will talk of his own coming death with a gentle patience that seems to cast out all fear.

80

XI

The Broken Tribes

NE of the effects of this earlier decimation of the people was a scattering of all of the Indians of the Lower
Columbia River Valley. They fled from their
homes and temporarily settled in any place that
provided them with the means of livelihood or
that promised exemption from the plague that
afflicted them. In this way the Cathlamets, whose
home was originally upon the Oregon side of
the Columbia River, below Puget Island, after
wanderings that are not recorded, finally settled
upon the present site of Cathlamet and near the
place of the ancient Indian town, and from this
people the modern town derives its name.

The Wahkiakums, who lived in the ancient

Indian village on the Elokomon Slough, near Cathlamet, returned to the ancient townsite after the panic was over, but only to leave it shortly after the coming of the Lewis and Clark expedition. This people gave their name to the County of Wahkiakum, within which Cathlamet is situated. What final catastrophe compelled the Wahkiakums to leave their ancient village is not known, but charred timbers and burned and blackened soil on the site of the old town point almost certainly to fire as the final scourge of the Indians on the Elokomon Slough.

These fragments of the Wahkiakum and Cathlamet peoples took up their homes together on the main Columbia River about one mile East of the old Indian village. Here they built their cedar houses and founded what is now the modern village of Cathlamet.

82

THE BROKEN TRIBES

What took place near Cathlamet must have taken place all over Western Oregon. Panic-stricken for the time the native people wandered about for several years, and fragments only of the ancient tribes returned to their old seats.

With this dispersion came an almost total disappearance of the tribal bonds and relationships. Every little settlement became a law to itself, and in Western Oregon there were no sharply defined tribal ties or boundaries. These peoples, as the white men came in, were gradually given the names of the localities in which they were found, or, as often happened, the locality was given the name of the principal Indian man who was found there, and afterwards the resident people were known by the same name. Thus, Wahkiakum was a chief of the

Cathlamets, and yet two tribes have apparently derived their names, one from the chief and one from the locality. These two tribes came together, and the double name, Wahkiakum-Cathlamet, is now perpetuated in the modern County of Wahkiakum and Village of Cathlamet. The building up of Indian names for modern use was a wondrous process, and no man knows just how it was done.

The Chinooks, Clatsops, Cathlamet-Wahkiakums and Coweliskies, with the native people of the Lower Willamette Valley, in this later period, roamed up and down the Columbia and Willamette Rivers between the Cascades of the Columbia and the Falls of the Willamette on the East, and the ocean on the West, and individuals of any tribe took up their residence at any place that pleased them, and in this way a good deal of mingling of the Indians took place.

With this dispersion of the Indians came an absolute failure in chieftainship. From 1800 on to the end it is remarkable how barren the lower river was of chiefs.

Comcomly, of the Chinooks; Chenamus, of the Clatsops; Wahkiakum, of the Cathlamets, and Umtux, of the Coweliskies, are the only four borne in remembrance, and of these Wahkiakum is known from a line or two in Washington Irving and as the founder of Cathlamet, while Umtux emerges from obscurity only by reason of his tragical end at the battle-ground back of Fort Vancouver during the Indian war of 1855-56.

Comcomly was more nearly a chief than any other Indian on the Columbia West of the Cascades, and this Duncan McDougall recognized in 1813 when he married one of his daughters. Many other Indians are named as chiefs in the books, and some of them may have had some claim to the title, but early historians called any principal man of the natives a chief. In fact, from the time of Cartier's voyage, in 1535, when a quaint old historian, writing of the Indian town of Hochelaga, on the St. Lawrence, speaks of meeting an Indian, "one of the principal lords of the said city," to 1608, when in the Long Wigwam of Wesowocomoco, the mighty Emperor Powhattan, was divested of his greasy raccoon robe and gowned and crowned in kingly style by the English, up to the present time, very erroneous ideas have prevailed in regard to the power and authority of Indian chiefs.

In time of war they were allowed a little

86

authority, but not much. In Eastern Oregon, where chiefs were plenty, they were without authority in time of peace, beyond the influence of their personal wealth and character, and on the lower river the villages were without law or authority from any native source.

During the latter days of Indian Cathlamet, Quillis was the principal man of the village, and had the largest lodge and family, and in earlier times would have been called a chief, but poor Quillis squabbled and scrambled with his brother Indians on terms of perfect equality, and if a canoe was to be hired or any contract made, his word was no better than that of anyone else.

XII.

The White Chiefs

HILE this confusion was at its height a new element came in, so wedded to the Indian life that it became part and parcel of it, and lived and died with it.

When in 1670 the "Governor and Company of Adventurers of England trading into Hudson's Bay," commenced to trade as the Hudson's Bay Company with North America, they had no purpose of founding a dynasty, and yet that is what they did: the dynasty of the chiefs of the Indian people.

Good old Dr. John McLoughlin, at Vancouver, was in all essential things a chief of the Indian people. His authority on the Columbia West of the Cascades was absolute, and it ex-

tended with varying power over the entire region
North of California and West of the Rocky
Mountains. His word was law to a lawless people, and the great chief was known as such
among all the Indians. He had all the characteristics of a chief — a quick temper, an arbitrary
will and the heart and the head of a governor
of men. He lived in impressive pomp, and all
down the river the story of the stately halls and
the wealth and magnificence of Fort Vancouver
was told by Indian to Indian with bated breath.

The present generation can never fully realize that Fort Vancouver was once in this Northwest country, the court of a King, and that poor
Indians wandering chieftainless and alone
looked to it as a center of power, culture and
wealth. In the lodges of Cathlamet, the Indian
mothers told their children of the wonderful

place and of the wealth of red blankets, of gay silk handkerchiefs and of powder and shot and provisions that were to be found in its store-houses.

The affection and respect of the Indians for McLoughlin was quickened by the fact of his having a wife of the Indian blood, who bore herself in her relations to her husband and the world as the wife of an Indian chieftain should. How much of the blood of this good woman was French or Scottish and how much Ojibway Indian nobody knows, but she carried herself as an Indian woman, and when visitors were at Fort Vancouver, effaced herself in true Indian fashion; loved and respected of her husband and of every one, she, according to common report, never presumed at Fort Vancouver to sit at her husband's table in the presence of strangers, and

90

in this, according to Indian notions, was only rendering due respect to her lord and master.

No requirement of Indian etiquette was more imperative than this, that an Indian woman should not be seen eating with her husband. It was her duty to wait upon and serve him, and afterwards provide for herself. It made no difference how wealthy she was, or how many servants she might have to wait upon her, she never presumed to put herself upon an equality with her husband or to be served before him. This was not an invariable rule, as more than one Indian woman took her place at the head of her white husband's table and there welcomed his guests, but this was not common and was generally confined to Indian women married from tribes East of the Rocky Mountains.

There are wives of the Indian blood now living on the Lower Columbia whose husbands
are well-to-do, influential men, who are loved
and respected of their husbands, who have the
respect of the communities in which they are
known, and who live handsomely and well, yet
who will not to this day sit at their own boun-
tiful and well-appointed tables with their husband and his guests. This native shyness and
reserve it is almost impossible for the native
women to give up, and it enhanced Dr. Mc-
Loughlin's dignity in the eyes of the natives
that his wife treated him as a chief.

XIII.

Indian Wives

THE relation of the white chiefs of the Hudson's Bay Company with native women presents a point of vivid interest in Indian history. For twenty years Fort Vancouver, like all other Hudson's Bay posts, was the home of fair-faced men and dark-faced women.

There is no doubt as to the standing of the women. They had been wedded in the ancient and orderly fashion of their people and in the forum of conscience were as much married as ever Queen Victoria was. They knew that their husbands could dismiss them at any time, but this was the ancient and inalienable right of the husband according to Indian ideas, and so with-

93

out a thought or care for the future they gladly
gave themselves to their white masters and
made loving and dutiful wives, and being used
to the country and at home, made very effective
helpmeets. The men accepted them upon the
same terms and not one man in ten dreamed at
first of the relation becoming a permanent one.
They were not of the class of the settlers, and
each man expected in due time to return to
England and there marry and found a family.

Some of them did dismiss their Indian wives.
There were two ways of doing this. One was
to pass the wife, often with a bonus of goods
or furs, over to some other white man; and this
although a cruel process, was much more mer-
ciful than the other, which was to send the
woman back to her own people.

No one who has ever seen an Indian wife

94

of a white man sent back to her people ever wanted to see such a thing again. Sorrowfully gathering up her little belongings, lingering over the task as long as possible, the poor dumb creature would finally come to the last parting. Without outcry or struggle she would try to accept her fate. One or two good-bye kisses, for the Indian women under the training of the white men soon learned to kiss, and then with her little bundles she would make her way back to the lodges.

For days and weeks she would bring little gifts of berries and game and lay them on her husband's doorstep, and for days and weeks would haunt the trading post or humbly stand near her husband's house, where he could see her, not daring to ask to be taken back, only hoping that his mood might change and that she might again be restored to her old place.

Resolute men broke down under the strain of such partings and took back their dusky wives for better or for worse until death should them part.

With the higher class of Hudson's Bay man the original marriage relation was very rarely dissolved. Little by little the light shone in upon him. Seeing at last clearly what he had done and strengthened by love of wife and children after many soul struggles, he faced his duty nobly, and calling in the minister took upon himself the marriage vows that bound him as well as the woman.

Dr. McLoughlin was married after the English fashion in 1836, eleven years after he and his wife had come to Fort Vancouver. Sir James Douglas was married at the same time, while

96

another prominent Hudson Bay man and his wife were joined together in the white man's fashion by the same minister that married their daughter to her husband and at the same time.

Romance treats it lightly, but whole tragedies of self-renunciation were bound up in many of these marriages.

Before McLoughlin came to Oregon another servant of the Hudson's Bay Company had been exercising all the functions and authority of a chief of the Indians. James Birnie was in every respect an interesting character, and had great influence with the Indians of the Columbia River, and from 1846 to his death in 1864 he lived and with his wife reigned at Cathlamet. He connected himself with the Hudson's Bay Company at Montreal, and three years later, in 1820, established a Hudson's Bay

97

Company post at The Dalles. He was at Fort Simpson in British Columbia, where one of the islands outside the harbor now bears his name, and afterwards was in charge of Fort George, now Astoria, at the mouth of the Columbia River.

In 1846 he severed his connection with the Hudson's Bay Company and settled in Cathlamet, the first white man to make a home there. Here he and his wife ruled in state and conducted what was in all essential particulars a post of the Hudson's Bay Company. The square Hudson's Bay store just east of the present steamboat landing at Cathlamet still stands. At least it is in the same position and is of the same shape, but clapboards and paint have given it a modern appearance. The old Birnie house was on the crest of the hill just back of the store. Like McLoughlin, Mr. Birnie had an Indian wife, brought with him from the Red River Indians of the East; but she, unlike Mrs. McLoughlin, bore herself with all the self-assertion of an English dame of long pedigree. She entertained in her own home and sat at the head of her own table, and no social center in those days in all the country was more fashionably attended than that of Mrs. Birnie. Once only in the year did she resume her Indian character, and that was for her annual trip to Shoalwater Bay for elk meat, clams and cranberries.

Mrs. Birnie's canoe was one of the wonders of the lower river. No larger one in the memory of Indians had ever been seen there. It was said that it could carry seventy people. In the fall of the year this canoe, manned by twenty or thirty Indian men and women, with all their belongings and household furniture aboard, would start seaward from Cathlamet.

Mrs. Birnie, all fire and energy, would be in command, and no woman on the river could command better. To the dip of the paddles and the Indian chant, the big canoe, enforcing respect everywhere, would pass the Chinook villages into Chinook River to the portage. Here the expedition would be taken over to the Nasel River and from there would pass into Shoalwater Bay. After a few weeks of hunting and fishing the party, with its spoils, would return by the same route.

Disposing of her gatherings and scattering her party, Mrs. Birnie would doff her Indian character and again assume her role as the grand dame of Birnie hall.

Here was one of the great gathering places of the lower river, and here at the wedding of Mrs. Birnie's daughters were gathered imposing assemblies. Thomas Fielding Scott, first missionary bishop of Oregon, an imposing figure in full canonicals, performed the marriage ceremonies. The Indians looked on in awe and amazement, and for weeks afterwards the little Indians gave dress rehearsals of the white man's wedding. The white robes of the bishop, which in their untutored way they took to be a glorified nightgown or white blanket in some way peculiarly appropriate for weddings, particularly took their fancy. To see a dirty little brat of an Indian with a piece of old cloth on, through rents in which gleamed a brown little stomach, attempt to repeat the marriage ceremony to a couple of other little brats, was very funny.

XIV.

Keeping the Peace

NEITHER Mr. Birnie nor any of the Hudson Bay employees had any legal authority over the Indians; law in these very early days was chiefly conspicuous for its absence, but each and every one of them fearlessly assumed the duty of a chief bound to maintain order within the bounds of his jurisdiction. Occasionally Dr. McLoughlin would have an Indian murderer hanged, and he never permitted any serious offense to go unpunished, but severe measures were rarely necessary.

Occasionally a naval expedition was sent out, but these on the lower river were not very destructive. George B. Roberts, Dr. McLoughlin's

Prime Minister at Vancouver, who in the latter
part of his life lived and finally died at Cathlamet, and who knew more of affairs at Vancouver and of the Indians than almost any one
else, had many comical tales to tell of these ex-
peditions. The irate old doctor would storm
about and order the instant punishment of the
offending Chinooks. If the armed schooner
Cadboro was away another little schooner would
be hauled to the bank and a big gun would
with infinite difficulty be transferred from the
fort to her deck, where it would be carefully
balanced to prevent an upset. Then in charge of
a flotilla of canoes the schooner with the great
black gun looming up impressively on the forward deck would proceed down the river to the
great awe and astonishment of all the Indians
until opposite the Chinook town, where she

would come to anchor. After allowing a sufficient time for every Chinook to get well away the big gun would be carefully trained upon a spot where good old Roberts thought there was no danger of hitting anybody and fired several times. A few houses would be knocked down and a few canoes would be captured. The Indians would make restitution and the principal offenders would receive some slight punishment. Then Dr. McLoughlin and Birnie and Roberts and the others would be again indulgent chiefs of their weak and erring people, and the Hudson's Bay Company would again enfold them with its protection. The schooner victorious, big gun and all, would sail up the river amidst great rejoicing and promptly resume its peaceful business of carrying goods and furs.

The chief instrument of discipline was the

store, for here every Indian was well known, and
he could trade to such extent only as the factor
allowed. If for any reason he was on the black
list for offenses unatoned for it made no difference how many beaver skins he could produce.
There was no sugar or tobacco, powder, shot
or blankets for him. In serious cases the store
would be entirely closed to the whole people
and this would bring the most stubborn tribe
to its knees, for without powder and shot they
were helpless, and without sugar and tobacco
they were miserable. All hunting and fishing
would stop, and about the storehouse would
be gathered, stolid but unhappy groups of Indian men and women squatting on the ground
and discussing the situation.

Finally a subdued and repentant committee
of the principal men would wait upon the of-

fended factor. They would be received with severe and impressive dignity, would very likely be kept waiting for several days for an interview with the chief. When admitted to his presence their business would be curtly and sternly demanded of them. Then a great silence would prevail; not a word would be said perhaps for half an hour or more. Finally a principal man would rise in his place and mournfully lay before the factor the unhappy condition of his people, carefully refraining from mentioning what he and the factor and everybody else knew was the secret of the whole trouble. Then the factor upon his part would curtly tell them what they all very well knew, that at such a time and place a white trapper had been robbed of his furs and outfit, and that until these had been returned and the criminals given up for punishment his heart was angry towards them, and that there were no goods for any one until restitution had been made.

After expressing their astonishment at the news and denying all knowledge of the affair and any ability to detect or bring in the offenders, the Indian committee would slowly stalk out, and the groups about the store would begin again their subdued conversations.

After a day or two some of the plundered goods would be returned. The factor would be obdurate. Then more would come in. Still the factor shook his head. After awhile all would be returned and the solemn committee would ask for mercy, and would plaintively tell that the robbers were of another tribe; that they had gone to a far-off illihee, etc., etc., but all in vain.

After a few days more Indian Jim and Indian Joe and their associates would be produced as the culprits. In nearly every case the offenders would surrender themselves to justice when the pressure on their people became sufficiently hard, but if not they were brought in by force.

Indians acted very much as children do, and one of their peculiarities was that a criminal seemed unable to keep silent regarding his crime, and however disastrous the consequences might be to himself, was compelled to confess and give himself up.

As one by one the Hudson's Bay Company gave up its posts the men who were foot loose returned to English soil, but many were not so free. Dr. McLoughlin and James Birnie, happy in their married life, were nevertheless not in a position to return home, and were compelled to stay in the wilderness with their wilderness people, and this was true of hundreds of others. Ties carelessly assumed at first, in the end held these men captives by a chain that they could not and would not break.

Already men and women are proud of the Indian blood in their veins, and more and more this feeling will grow, but at this early time the Indian wife could only be happy in her native land, and was unfitted for any other; and it speaks well for the great hearts of these noble men that they recognized this and gave themselves a willing sacrifice to a new country and a dying race. They had connected themselves with a changing time and were compelled to change and pass away with it.

The clinging arms of the wilderness women were about them and held them to their forest life. There they lived and there they died, and the God of the wilderness has pronounced their work good.

XV.

Chief Umtux

MENTION has been made of the peaceful character of the Indians along the Lower Columbia and their broken strength. It is a fact, therefore, to be noticed that after Fort Vancouver came into the possession of the Americans a number of these Indians did on one occasion form line of battle against the whites, and that by reason of what then happened one spot in the Lower Columbia River Valley bears to this day the title of a battle ground.

The Coweliskies who lived on the Cowlitz River, then known as the Coweliskie, and along the two branches of the Lewis River in what is now known as Cowlitz and Clark Counties of the State of Washington, were not of the pure river type of Indian, nor did they live directly on the banks of the Columbia. They had a trail extending from the Cowlitz River to the gravel plains South of Olympia, Tacoma and Seattle. Some of them who lived near the Gravel Plains had ponies and were what might be called half horse and half canoe Indians. They were a more lively and warlike people than the Chinooks and held a middle position between the Columbia River and the Puget Sound Indians.

Indians are by nature great gamblers, and it is hard where all so excelled to specify any one tribe that was preeminent in this fascinating vice, but perhaps the Indians of the Lower Puget Sound country were entitled to this award. Too timorous to go to actual war and take chances with death, they were also too

112

adventurous to be contented in mere eating and drinking, and therefore gambled with an abandon that put to shame the very best modern efforts of our gilded youth. The white man plays to some limit, but these Indians had none.

Whenever any of these Indian communities on Puget Sound acquired enough portable property to make it worth while they sent out invitations to their neighbors for a meeting at some appointed place, and to this spot the Indians would flock from every point of the compass. They would bring with them their wives, children, dogs, horses, furs, robes, weapons and every bit of their property that they could carry along, leaving nothing at home except their canoes and lodges. The prominent features of these aboriginal fairs or expositions were what might be called "agricultural horse trots."

Horse racing as a gambling game was an institution amongst them, and every little community of the horse Indians had its racing pony, which was at once its pride and hope. Other gambling games were played at these meetings but the horse race was the greatest of them all. Curiously enough the Indian in his native state never raced canoes. This is a modern invention of the white man.

To these race meets appointed by the Indians of Lower Puget Sound many of the Coweliskies with their wives and chattels would go, and generally they came back afoot without their chattels and sometimes without their wives.

Upon the speed of their favorite pony the Indians would stake everything: robes, goods and horses, and, the fever of gambling upon them, would not hesitate to stake and lose the

clothing from off their backs or even their faithful squaws.

This betting of a wife upon a gambling
game was a rare event, not because of any disinclination on the part of the loving husband
to put up the wife of his bosom on a wager,
but rather to the disinclination of the other man
to put up anything of value against such skit-
tish property as Indian squaws. The Indian
might be a gambler, but he wasn't always a
fool, and to win an assorted lot of wives was
not exactly the way to get rich or happy.

It was only in cases like that of the amorous
Jewish King that an Indian would in a gambling game put up anything of value against an
Indian woman, and had King David and his
faithful Uriah been Columbia River Indians,
the wily old lover would have needed only to

put his faithful soldier in the front of a poker game to get his wife, and the putting of Uriah in the front of the battle and the shedding of blood would have been spared the Psalmist.

This intercourse of the Coweliskies and the Puget Sound Indians naturally made them friendly, and when the Indian war of 1855-56 was in progress and Chief Leschi on the Sound was taking the Puget Sound Indians into war with the whites, great fear was felt on the Columbia River that the Coweliskies would be drawn into the conflict, and it was deemed best to keep them at Fort Vancouver, and there they were brought and kept in semi-imprisonment.

At this time the regulars were in the field, and a company of volunteers was, greatly to its dissatisfaction and to the dissatisfaction of its Captain, in garrison at Fort Vancouver, and the fort was the center of more general alarms and troubles than any other point in the Northwest. The Yakima Indians were attacking the Cascades settlement only thirty miles to the Eastward, and a large number of settlers had been killed there. General, then Lieutenant Philip Sheridan, with only forty men, the last of the regulars, had gone to the Cascades to withstand them, and was having a hard time. Everywhere fear was about Vancouver and all of the settlers from the threatened points were encamped about it for protection.

Panics were of daily happening and it was a common occurrence for such a panic to arise in some strange way in the middle of the night. A cry would be raised in the darkness that the Indians were coming, and in a moment the muddy roads and trails through the dark woods would be thronged with the panic-stricken people fleeing to the fort for protection. Most of the men were absent at the front fighting Indians, but the trampling women and children had a hard time of it, and the few men stationed at the fort, and especially the young Captain, had almost more than they could do to keep order and still remain in a posture of defense against the very real Indian enemy only thirty miles away.

Amidst all of these alarms the camp of the Coweliskies lay like a dark cloud under the fort, portending danger, and many a mother and many a fighting man, looking at it with apprehension, wished that it might be destroyed before it broke and scattered, carrying fire and death with it.

118

While things were in this condition the Coweliskies suddenly decamped. In a single night their camp disappeared and in the morning the settlers saw in their fancy their worst fears confirmed: the Coweliskies had gone on the warpath and now the Indian war was to be brought to their own firesides.

The company was promptly put under arms and went in pursuit, and about fifteen miles Northwest of Vancouver overtook the fugitives. Great difficulty was found in locating them and still greater difficulty in finding out their intentions, whether for war or peace. To precipitate a conflict by striking the Indians unnecessarily would in the unprotected condition of the settlers have been a crime, while to let the Indians escape to carry on in unbroken force an Indian warfare would have been worse.

The young Captain placed his little force across the path of the Indians and went to work to develop the situation. Negotiations were entered into. The two forces stood on their guard against each other, but everything went well, and one evening the Indians finally promised to return the next morning, and for the first time for many nights the young Captain had rest. In that night some lawless idiot did his deadly work, and the next morning it was learned that Umtux, the chief of the Indians, lay dead between the lines. Who killed him no one knows or suspects to this day. None of the sentrys fired upon him and none of his Indians appeared to have had murder against him in their hearts. Nevertheless there lay Chief Umtux half way between the lines of his people and the lines of the volunteers, indubitably very dead. Lying in the trail by the side of a log with the hole made by a rifle bullet through him, Chief Umtux was more dangerous dead than living, and instantly the battle lines were formed in earnest and for a few hours Chief Umtux lay upon the crimsoned soil of what it seemed would at last be a genuine battle-ground of Northwestern Oregon. Steadily the two forces stood against each other, but fortunately no other shot was fired and Western Oregon was spared an Indian war.

A brave French voyageur volunteered to go to the Indians and resume treaty-making, and taking his life in his hands stood in their midst. It is told that it was a dramatic scene. The Indians, half crazed with fear and lust of revenge, stood about him. He explained as he best could that the death of Umtux was not the act of the soldiery, but of some lawless ranger, and that if they would submit they would be protected. Gradually with perfect skill and fearlessness he won back their confidence and obtained a renewal of their promise to go back to the fort.

One strange thing for Indians, they stipulated for, and that was that the soldiers should return and leave them free for twenty-four hours to bury their chief unobserved. When this condition was reported to the young Captain he was doubtful. On the one hand it looked like an Indian trick to escape without a battle, while on the other hand their Chief had been unfairly killed and they had a just right to suspect the good faith of the white men.

After some hours of consideration he accepted the solemn promise of the Indians and marched his men back to the fort, leaving the

Coweliskies alone with their dead. Chief Umtux was buried that night, but how and where no man save his Indians ever knew, and they never told.

If you will look upon a map you will see a place about twelve or fifteen miles Northeast of Vancouver that bears to this day the name of "Battleground." Near here the Indians stood at bay, and near here Umtux was buried.

The death of Umtux was a direct blow at the peace that then prevailed between the Indians and the white men in Western Oregon, and his murder was an act of violence that disgraces the pioneer annals of Oregon, but there was more to come, and what happened afterwards shows in still another light the less noble side of the pioneer character, for the pioneer men had the faults of their virtues. Their boldness sometimes became temerity, their love of liberty license, and their justice revenge, and the wife of the pioneer was like unto him.

When the company came marching back into the fort without any Indians either dead or alive and without a battle to report, excitement ran high and when it became known upon what terms they had allowed the Indians to remain, the excitement increased. There could be no talk of lynching, because the company contained practically all the fighting men of the settlement, so the women with busy tongues took the matter into their own hands, and when the company was assembled, appeared before it, and, in the presence of an excited crowd, presented to the Captain a woman's red petticoat as a banner for his soldiers. It was a deadly insult and the company quailed under it.

For a moment matters looked serious, and there was every prospect of a general riot and a free fight, but the Captain was a man of parts and equal to the situation. With a white face he stepped forward and on behalf of his company accepted the gift. In a few manly words he told the women and the gaping crowd that they did not know what they did or appreciate the reason for the action of the soldiers, and assured them that if it should be the good fortune of the company to be ordered to the front that their flag would be carried into action, and if so carried would be dyed a deeper red before it returned, and then turning to his company gave a short military command. There was some hesitation in obeying it, and a tall, lanky fellow made some insolent remark and drew a bowie knife. That was enough, and with joy in his heart that his wrath could be unloosed and that he had somebody besides women to expend his anger upon, in one bound the Captain was upon him. The man made one ineffectual stroke with his knife, and ever after one side of the Captain's mouth, where the knife cut in, drooped under his moustache a little more than the other, and then the man went down helpless as a child in a grasp that threatened to choke out life.

The Captain always afterwards cheerfully insisted that he was only maintaining military discipline, and would not have killed the man, but the men of his company, in telling of the affair, claimed that they saved the fellow's life only by pulling the Captain off. The Captain stood six feet two inches in his stockings and had had provocation that would have angered an angel,

126

so perhaps the truth was with the rank and file.

The next day, true to their appointment, the Coweliskies came marching in and put themselves under the protection of the white Captain, and the women with one of those swift revulsions of feeling that follow so fast after heedless action, were profuse in their apologies and wanted to take back their flag; besides the woman who had lent the petticoat wanted it back for personal reasons, for petticoats were short in more ways than one in those days, but no, the members of the company were obdurate. The petticoat had been given to them and their flag it would remain.

The Coweliskies made no more trouble. The Indian war rolled Eastward back from the gates of the Cascades. The settlers went home and confidence was restored. Then the company was disbanded, taking back with it only the satisfaction of knowing that it had done its duty and that it had been the only military command of the war that had been presented with a banner.

The Coweliskies in their squalor were but a poor and far away imitation of the angels that buried the great law giver, yet their work abides, for of Umtux it is true "that no man knoweth of his sepulchre unto this day."

XVI.

Happy Days

HERE were few more joyful or ani-
mated sights than a lodge or hunting
party of Indians in good luck. The
Indian bucks sitting around smoking or gambling, the Indian women busy in preserving fish
and meat and preparing skins, and the funny
little children and the dogs: a mingled, whoop-
ing, joyful mass, eating, sleeping and playing
all day long. Even the little baby with his tightly
bound head and body strapped to a board hung
up against a tree, looked around with his little
beady eyes in contented amusement, and unless
frightened never cried.

Amongst themselves or with their intimate
friends they were not at all reserved, but joked

and told stories with the utmost freedom. Many of these stories, told in the open lodge before the women and children, would not bear repeating, could not well pass inspection for the Government mail.

As the lingering remnant of this people approached the end, on one conspicuous occasion Providence threw a broad gleam of sunshine over their path and made all of them rich beyond the utmost dreams of Indian avarice.

In 1861 came a day when the snows gathered and the rains fell. The Clackamas, Molalla, Santiam, and McKenzie, the Long Tom, Rickreall, Yamhill and Tualatin poured their crowded waters into the Willamette River and swept it with a great flood from end to end. Linn City, opposite Oregon City, was swept away to the bedrock, and flouring mills, saw mills, warehouses, wharves, stores and houses from all along the river went floating to the sea in a mass. The Columbia River at Cathlamet was covered for days with lumber, flour, furniture and property of every description, and the tides there made salvage easy.

Every Indian and every canoe along the river was busy. Flour was the principal thing saved. This wets in only about half an inch, and remains just as good as ever inside.

In front of the Quillis lodge was ranged a great pile of sacked flour, food enough for years. Lumber was brought ashore in any quantity that was wanted. The Indians even tied up a whole wharf and warehouse in one of the sloughs below the town.

They saved furniture and clothing and crockery, everything that an Indian could ask

131

for. Incalculable wealth rolled along for days on the river and the Indians were free to pick and choose. The little Indians whooped along the bank with their loose, single shirt half the time over their heads and never covering their nakedness.

"Nanich! nanich!" (see! see!) they shouted, and *"Hiyu supalil! hiyu supalil!"* (plenty flour! plenty flour!) dancing up and down in their excitement and occasionally making a wild plunge toward the river to save some article that floated near shore, occasionally, too, falling in and being pulled out and slapped by the watchful, excited mothers.

It was almost incredible what came down the river. There was no rattlesnake country within 150 miles, and yet an old log house came floating by alive with rattlesnakes. Bales of hay

132

floated by with crowing chickens. One young Indian attracted by the neat look of some white painted beehives that came floating by on the platform of on old outhouse, took one aboard his canoe. A moment after he went howling overboard, and when he was pulled ashore and emptied of the water that had poured into him, expressed his opinion in unvarnished terms of the white people who put up hornets in white boxes. *"Hiyu Mesatchie,"* and then, as the Indian vocabulary failed, "D---n *Mesatchie."* As for the beehive and the canoe, they went sailing out over the bar, and so far as any one knows, these bees are the same ones that are now making the beeswax that washes up every now and then from the Pacific Ocean.

It was a gorgeous time, and when the flood of wealth was over the Indians of the lower river were richer than they had ever been even in their dreams.

To Quillis and his people, however, the inquiry that suggested itself to the sportsmen who found four pounds of bread and ten gallons of whisky in their camp luggage, soon suggested itself, "What did they want so much bread for?" A lot of flour was promptly exchanged for a sixty-gallon barrel of whisky, and Ingersoll never sang the song of the oaken barrel half as joyously as the Indians did.

It was the last great feast of the Columbia River Indians. Only one thing marred its joyousness and this was temporary. Old Quillis was a wise old chap, and as the whisky brightened up his intellect it occurred to him that the barrel of whisky would last one Indian longer than it would the tribe, so he quietly stole the

134

half empty cask and hid it in the woods, but Quillis sober could not find what Quillis drunk had hidden, so after a week of antics that alarmed the rest of his tribe as to his sanity, Quillis called his people together and confessed his sin and begged their help in finding the precious barrel. After a long search enthusiastically joined in by all the Indians, the barrel was found and the interrupted feast went on.

Gradually the race died out, happy in the Indian fashion, and care-free to the last, and the survivors in the Willamette Valley and the Valley of the Columbia can now almost be counted on the fingers. They did not pass away unnoticed or alone. Other powers and noted men tied to them in the web of fate, passed away with them. Great captains of the imperial race sat in their lodges, and a President, to be, of the United States, traveled in somewhat sorry state in their canoes, in those last few years.

XVII.

The Pioneers

O PICTURE of the Western Indian can be complete without reference to the race that supplanted him and the circumstances of the contact of the two races so long as it existed.

> Shuffle Shoon and Amber Locks
> Sit together building blocks,
> Shuffle Shoon is old and gray,
> Amber Locks a little child.

> One speaks of the long ago,
> Where his dead hopes buried lie,
> One with chubby cheeks aglow,
> Prattleth of the By and By.

In 1850 there were probably not to exceed one thousand white men in all the vast district lying North of the Columbia River. The Willamette Valley South of the Columbia, was comparatively well settled with white people, but from Cathlamet Northward for thousands of miles the wilderness lay unmarked by white men's hands.

A few hamlets on Puget Sound, a house at Cathlamet, another at Oak Point and a few others here and there, with Fort Vancouver, was all.

Cathlamet was one of the loneliest places on the earth. Into its loneliness in 1850 came a white pioneer and his wife, with two little babies. A trail through the woods was made to the point on the river about a quarter of a mile below Mr. Birnie's, and here a small log house was built and occupied.

It is hard to conceive of the impulse or instinct that brought two such people into such a situation. The man was a trained lawyer, as after events made clear, one of the highest types of his profession. Even before he left the East his abilities were recognized, and he stood on equal terms with men who in the stirring events of the next ten years were to earn world-wide fame. He was a man of culture and refinement.

At a time when college graduates were rarer than they are now, he was a graduate of Yale College, and always bore about him the evidence of his training. Greek was familiar to him, and Latin he could read to the end of his days almost as readily as he could English. Not only college bred, but a man of wide and choice reading, he made a strange selection of a place for the exercise of his undoubted talents and capabilities, but, strange as was his choice of a

139

home, it was a still more strange home for his wife, who for some years was the only white woman of Cathlamet.

A refined and cultivated young woman, thoroughly educated and accustomed to the best social circles of the Eastern States, with two little babies, was somewhat out of place in the Cathlamet of 1850. The pioneer instinct is one of the strangest instincts of a virile race, and no stranger manifestation of it ever appeared than this. In the long Winter nights the wolves howled within hearing of the little log house, and the young women of today, fearful of a mouse, would not have thought it a cheerful sound. With wolves on one side and an Indian village on the other, the bravest of women might have felt a little timid.

The first few years at Cathlamet were years

of hardship for this white family. The duties of the man compelled him to be away from home and to be at Oregon City, Salem and other points a great portion of the time, and his wife was left alone with her children.

His income was ridiculously small, and was almost consumed in traveling and similar expenses, so that the improvement of the place grew very slowly, and household comforts were not to be had, and the surroundings made the young wife's position a very hard one.

One of the peculiarities of Indian life is the little apparent effect that an Indian village has upon wild animals in its proximity. The large gray wolf, the most knowing and elusive of animals, will loiter around the outskirts of an Indian village, and upon occasions will come into it almost as fearlessly as the native dogs. It may be that the wolfish nature of the Indian dogs invites such familiarity, but there is no love lost between the wolf and the dog, and it is not uncommon for the wolves to kill and eat their dog brethren.

In Metlakahtla, a large Indian village of eight hundred people, on Annette Island, in Alaska, two years ago, large gray wolves came, even in Summer nights, into the heart of the town, and the shadowy gray creatures were frequently met with on the streets. Wolves would not have come within five miles of a town of equal size of white people.

Wild animals fairly swarmed about Cathlamet.

Every now and then a choice duck of the tame flock would be heard squawking loudly and be seen progressing across the sloughs in a direction in which he evidently did not want to go. A cunning little mink had seized him from below and was towing him off. Not a sign of the mink could be seen, and when anybody shot at the sorrowful procession they generally killed the duck, and the mink went free.

The family pig, upon which was centered many hopes, would be feeding in a little pasture near the house, when a great hulking bear would come rolling over the fence and little piggy, with a frantic squeal issuing from one end of him, and his curly tail twisting frantically from the other, would disappear in the dark woods, never to be heard of more.

The cougars took toll from the dozens or so of sheep that were kept, and would come into the very corrals for that purpose.

As if this were not enough, the Indian dogs

took a hand in the sport and worried the sheep whenever they could, and nothing would persuade the Indians to reduce the number of their canine pests. The white men formed an impromptu protective association, and shot the dogs whenever they could catch them, until the dogs learned the trick of running into the lodges whenever they saw a white man around with a gun.

This protected them for some time, until the sheep were nearly gone, when something had to be done, and then one of the white men with a rifle in one hand for emergencies, and a Colt's revolver in the other for dogs, boldly went into the lodges and shot the dogs there. It was risky work.

The inside of the lodge was all smoky and confusion, and the children and the Indians

144

hid the dogs in the beds, but canine curiosity was too strong, and every now and then a dog would stick his head out and bark. Crack would go the revolver, half a dozen more dogs would break out simultaneously, and it would be bow-wow, crack, crack, until the revolver was empty.

In this way the dog pest was kept down and the sheep were given some chance for their lives.

There was naturally a very limited market, and not much variety in food, and salt salmon and potatoes grew tiresome.

The only thing that made living possible was that wild game was abundant and cheap. A few charges of gunpowder and shot would buy a fine wild duck or goose, a single charge of gunpowder would buy a forty-pound salmon, and an Indian would sometimes come in with his one-man canoe loaded with wild fowl, which he would sell for anything the white people would give for them.

The family grew larger, and as children were born to Mrs. Birnie and the young white wife, the white woman and the red would minister at each other's bedsides like sisters, and the friendships so formed never failed or changed so long as the two women lived.

Occasionally some relief came to the monotony. In 1853 a visit was made to Fort Vancouver, nearly a hundred miles away. To save expense the traveling was done in a canoe, with an Indian crew, and as a baby six months old was a necessary passenger on the journey, it will be seen how anxious this white woman was to see and talk with her own people again.

During all of this time at Cathlamet the In-

146

dians looked to the white woman for help in
every time of trouble. Was a native baby sick
the white mother must know some remedy; was
any Indian hurt the white woman in the absence
of the white man must do the necessary surgi-
cal work.

It was one continual demand, and the back
porch of the house was lined with Indians almost every morning with olallies (berries) to sell,
with ducks or geese to dispose of, or with some
tale of woe or sickness to tell. Generally one or
two Indian women were about the house help-
ing in some capacity, and their relatives would
visit them as often as they were allowed.

Indian women visiting were not enlivening
creatures. Coming in quietly with a hardly ar-
ticulate *"klowhiam"* or good morning, they
would stand around, saying nothing. When

147

pressed to stay, they would look about, chatter a little among themselves, and then, carefully avoiding the chairs, would curl their legs under them and squat down on the floor. Once there they were fixed to stay until told to go home.

The original Indian woman always squatted on the floor in preference to sitting on anything higher, and always stayed until she was told it was time to depart. She used her eyes a good deal, but her tongue very little.

As household help the Indian girls were quick to learn and ready to work, but so soon as they were educated to a point where they were useful and dressed nicely and kept clean, they became so attractive that they were married out of hand.

The household help by reason of this was

148

a continual succession of Indian Lucys, Margarets, etc., without number.

XVIII.

The Pioneer Mother

WITH visiting the sick, teaching the young and caring for her own family, the pioneer mother had her hands full, and of the fruits of her labor she saw but little. The life was terribly narrow, but so full of labor and danger that there was no time to repine. The coming of a white man with a white woman who settled in Elokomon Valley, about two miles back of Cathlamet, was a great event.

The low divide between the Columbia and Elokomon Rivers was covered at this time by a dense forest of the spruce and Douglas fir, and so thick was the growth that the fir trees would go up for 100 feet without a limb, and not a ray of the sun could reach the ground. The trees grew very tall, and one a short way outside the forest on the edge of a little prairie being measured with instruments, was found to be about 308 feet in height.

An almost obliterated Indian trail went over the divide between the rivers, and so anxious were the white women to see each other that it was a very common thing for them to go over it. One hundred yards up the trail there was nothing to see but trees, and one mile in the woods was as far away from human help as the wilds of Siberia.

One day when one of them with two of her little boys was on the trail in the midst of the woods, a large cougar suddenly appeared in it not forty yards away and stood looking at her. Now, the cougar is an uncanny beast, and in these Northern woods, a most formidable one. A man can live in the woods for years and never see one, and yet some day the supple yellow panther will stand in front of him on some woodland path as though he had come there by magic. Not a footfall or sound of breaking twig will give any warning of his coming. He will simply be there; it is a trick of his, and he always takes the same position, calmly looking at you without curiosity and without fear, very rarely if ever crouching, and growling, if at all, in a gentle, sing-song drawl, more like purring than anything else.

With a low flattened head, the little ears drawn back, softly poised on sinewy, tawny legs and velvet pads, and with the long sweeping tail gently going from right to left and left to right with a quiet, steady motion, the cou-

gar when he steps out of obscurity into the open
to observe man, is an impressive creature.

An armed man stops to consider a moment
before he fires, and an unarmed man has a very
lively desire to be somewhere else. Only in the
woods can you see a cougar so, and it is not a
pleasant sight for a woman with empty hands.

There was one best thing to do, and, prompted by the mother's instinct, this mother did it.
Taking one child by each hand and drawing
them close up to her, so as to present a united
front, she calmly looked the beast in the eyes
and slowly and steadily moved towards him.
She said it was the only thing that she could
very well do.

The grim lips curled back a little, and the
white teeth showed; but few animals unwound-
ed can face man, and, retiring step by step, the

cougar moved back before her, and gliding into the brush, disappeared.

An Indian woman would have stood in her place, and, gathering her children under her blanket, would have waited the issue in patience, and if forced into a fight, would have made a better one than the white woman; but steadily moving up into the face of the enemy was the English blood, and for cold-blooded courage when courage was necessary, the white woman was the superior of her red sister.

This was only one of many anxieties and perils. With so many burdens the children had largely to take care of themselves, and one day a two-year-old boy being missing, a search was instituted and the youngster was found floating in an eddy of the Columbia River, quietly clinging to a little piece of driftwood. He had fallen

154

over a rocky cliff about eight feet high into the river, and had found a natural life-preserver in the tiny piece of wood just at hand. Indian Margaret was the nurse then, and she quietly stripped herself, swam out like a duck and towed the baby in. Except for that friendly piece of driftwood and Indian Margaret, this little narrative would never have been written.

Another time of extreme anxiety was when the Indians had procured large supplies of liquor. A frightful hubbub would prevail in the Indian village, and as this was directly between the Strong and Birnie houses, it made a fearsome situation.

The Indians, harmless enough at ordinary times, were liable to be dangerous when drunk, and more than once the children were chased home by drunken Indians with drawn knives.

It was perhaps a drunken joke, but if so, the joking was on a very serious subject, and a white-faced little woman barring her doors and windows with only her small children within, had no enjoyment of the situation.

XIX.

The Red Box

HE Indian War of 1855-56 brought great anxiety to Cathlamet. There were a few more white men there then, but the preponderance of the Indian was still overwhelming, and when it became whispered about that the Klickitat Chief Kamiakin, the head and front of the war, had messengers at Cathlamet, there was fear everywhere, but the native Indians stood up manfully for their white friends, who had helped them, and Mrs. Birnie and her husband held them with a steady hand.

Here was one of the great advantages to the Hudson's Bay men of having Indian wives. No plotting could go on without their knowledge, and in a time of stress the Indian wife could always be relied on. No white person saw the messengers or knew who they were, but that they came was certain.

Across the little creek in a small pasture stood two tall spruce trees, and at the top of one of these, placed on a limb trimmed off for the purpose, suddenly appeared a large box, red as blood. There it remained for months, and even years, and was said to be Kamiakin's signal to war, but no white man knew how it got there or what its message was.

One explanation of its presence only deepens the mystery. If an Indian killed another he would, so it is claimed, procure a small box, paint it a brilliant red and attach it to a limb high upon some conspicuous tree, cutting close to the trunk all the limbs below it, and it is said that this in some strange way showed repentance for the crime and amounted to a punishment because the life of the murderer would only last so long as the box remained secure in its high place. As the box was generally very securely attached, the murderer's life was quite safe for many years, and no other Indian would meddle with it.

This particular red box that appeared so mysteriously at Cathlamet in the time of Kamiakin's war was, it is claimed, placed there by a son of the Chief of the Skookum Tillicums (Strong People), who had murdered a fellow-Indian and was intended by him as a public confession of guilt and an expiatory sacrifice.

Be this as it may, the mere suggestion opens up many strange phases of the Indian character. No Indian ever openly humilated himself, and if such a custom prevailed the elevation of the red box was made more in pride than in humility. "I have slain" it said, and no ordinary Indian had much compunction in this or thought it lowered him in the estimation of his fellows.

If the young Skookum Tillicum hoisted such a signal in the feverish times of a general war, and the settlers had known that he was boasting of an accomplished murder, it is more than likely that they would have taken it for granted that his message was, "I have slain, I have slain. Go thou and do likewise," and would probably have promptly disposed of young Skookum Tillicum.

This strange red box might well therefore have been a confession, a boast and a call to war all in one, and people as quick as are the

Indians in interpreting signs would very easily have known its deeper import, although they might not tell it to their white neighbors.

The red box raised high upon the tree did not add any to the comfort or feeling of security of the few white people that lived at Cathlamet.

From 1850 to 1862 the pioneer life of Cathlamet went on, the white population steadily increasing and the red as steadily diminishing.

The order of burial of the Book of Common Prayer was continually in use and was read over many lonely little graves, every trace of which has since been swept away.

One of the saddest of these burials was that of Indian George, a young Indian of sixteen. He had been a slave of the Tsimpseans, Northern Indians, from Fort Simpson, and on one of their insolent war excursions into Puget Sound, Judge Strong saw him, and, moved with pity at his deplorable condition, bought him for two dollars and fifty cents worth of goods and brought him to Cathlamet. Here he grew up in the household into a strong, happy boy, but every now and then the wild instinct would come upon him and he would run away. Nothing would be done to reclaim him, and in a few weeks he would return, ragged and thin, but very happy to get back. Nothing pleased him so much as to salute the little steamboats that used to come monthly from San Francisco by dipping to them a little home-made American flag, and when he lay dying of consumption his every wish was gratified by the promise that he should be buried shrouded in it.

162

XX.

The End

HE earlier Cathlamet life was sometimes enlivened by the visits of strangers, and one of these is worthy of
remembrance.

Half way between the Hudson's Bay store
and the Strong house was a little cove in the
low, rocky bank before which, in high tide,
floated the Indian canoes and behind which was
the Indian lodges. An old logging railway and
cannery wharves now hide it almost from sight,
but it was in this early day the principal landing place for the Indian village and here in
times past McLoughlin, McDougall, McTav-
ish and many other notables had landed.

In the Fall of 1852 a canoe turned in to the

163

landing from the Columbia River, and in it were an Indian crew and a rather short young man of pink and white complexion, evidently one of the new United States officers at Fort Vancouver. He was a stranger in the country and was on a trip to Shoalwater Bay and very anxious to get some white man to go on with him. He stayed at the Strong house for several days and so prevailed upon his host that at the end of his visit they went off together to the bay.

No record of this trip exists, and no official report of it was ever made. The Indians were reticent in regard to it, and all the two men vouchsafed to say was that they had had a jolly good time and would have stayed longer had the provisions held out.

Twice again the young officer came to Cath-

THE END

lamet a welcome guest, and then his short stay of a year in this country being finished, went away to the career that time had in store for him, and a marvelous career it was, for it was written in the book of fate that this obscure young Captain Grant should command the armies of the great Republic in the mightiest war of modern times, that he should sit as a ruler of the Nation and should finally sleep in that great tomb that looks down upon the Hudson.

It was fated that both host and guest should sleep at last at two Riversides far apart, one in his stately tomb by the Hudson, and the other under the trees and grass by the dark forest he loved so well, looking down upon the Willamette.

One rendered a great service to his country

in its time of need and met with quick and great reward; the other at the fountain head of the history of a great commonwealth, after the fashion of the pioneers, expended his life and strength for a coming people and gave of the best that was in him for future generations.

Another visitor was a dashing young fellow from New York who entered into wilderness life with a zest. For the few years he was here his adventures were numberless. When as clerk of the court in some fiercely contested murder or other case he carelessly unslung his revolver and sat at his desk with it lying on the table before him, there was order in the court, for everybody knew what he could do with fire-arms.

Only once did the wilderness get the advantage of him, and then he owed his life to

the friendly service of an Indian. While surveying a road from Cathlamet Northward to the
Boisfort Prairie, with the idea of extending it
to Puget Sound, he was, when a little away
from the party, suddenly charged upon by an
enraged elk.

Being without weapons, he dived for the
first place of shelter at hand, which happened
to be a small fallen tree lying about two feet
above the ground. The elk would furiously
strike at him with hoofs and horns on one side,
and would then jump over and strike at him
from the other, and the only way to avoid the
savage animal was to keep up a very alert dodg-
ing under the tree from side to side.

This game of hide and seek went on for several hours until the man was nearly worn out,
the elk growing more and more active and his

eyes growing greener and more furious, as their manner is when balked, until an Indian coming up shot him and allowed a very tired, dirty and humbled young man to limp back to camp.

It was written for this young man that he, too, should serve his country in the Civil War, but that less fortunate than some of his comrades, he should fall in battle at the head of his brigade, crippled for life by a shot through the hips.

As a white-haired old General he now walks haltingly in his vineyard in California, and thinks often of early Oregon and of the days when "all the world was young."

About the time of the great flood of 1861 came one of the coldest Winters ever known in Oregon, the Winter of 1861-62. Ice rarely forms at Cathlamet, but that Winter the water along the shores of the Columbia was frozen so solidly that horses and sleds were used on it, and snow fell and remained on the ground to the depth of three feet. The little steamer Multnomah, with genial Captain Hoyt as master, was frozen in at Cathlamet, and so were quite a number of other people.

There is at least one staid, elderly woman of Portland who will remember the gay carnival of that Winter in the white and Indian town of Cathlamet. The Indians had plenty of food and clothing and were happy. The whites were jolly, as pioneers always were if they had half a chance.

The six weeks of freezing weather was filled in with sleigh-riding, games and dancing, and from the hills of Cathlamet to the Columbia River the men, boys and women, white and

Indian, coasted continually. Food with the white people grew scanty, but this made no difference, and a fine young horse was shot for meat and served on the tables as roast beef.

In the log houses and the lodges great fires blazed and there was nothing of sorrow or fear, and so we end the story, for here Cathlamet ceases to be Indian Cathlamet, and became from this time on a town of the "Bostons."